Guerrilla Kindness

& Other Acts of Creative Resistance

Making A Better World Through Craftivism

Sayraphim Lothian

Cover and Layout Design: Elina Diaz
Photography: Sayraphim Lothian

For permission requests, please contact the publisher at:

Mango Publishing Group
2850 Douglas Road, 3rd Floor
Coral Gables, FL 33134 USA
info@mango.bz

For special orders, quantity sales, course adoptions and corporate sales, please email the publisher at sales@mango.bz. For trade and wholesale sales, please contact Ingram Publisher Services at customer.service@ingramcontent.com or +1.800.509.4887.

Guerrilla Kindness and Other Acts of Creative Resistance: Making A Better World Through Craftivism

Library of Congress Cataloging
ISBN: (paperback) 978-1-63353-740-8, (ebook) 978-1-63353-741-5
Library of Congress Control Number: 2018937913
BISAC category code : POL043000 — POLITICAL SCIENCE / Political Process / Political Advocacy

Printed in the United States of America

This book is dedicated to my husband Rob, because of everything.

*And to the memory of my grandmother Marjory Jane,
who taught me generosity and craft.*

"As a fat feminist mother, activist and artist, I've been actively participating in craftivism and using guerrilla kindness as a revolutionary way of making, creating, engaging, and resisting for nearly a decade. Women have been using traditional handiwork for generations to not only provide for their families and make a living, but to tell stories. Lothian's work and book provides a fun and tangible way to teach a new generation to continue this legacy while making it their own, not focusing on perfection but on crafting and art-making as a radical tool for change."

—**Amy Pence-Brown**, body image activist, historian, artist, and writer

"DIY craft and activism have gone together since well before the internet brought us images of radical quilts and seditious samplers. Yet now more than ever before craftivism is resonating with so many people, keen to truly make a difference in their communities and the world. Sayraphim Lothian's book is a must-read for anyone in need of inspiration and motivation to bring people together to make positive change. You'll be left mega inspired and raring to engage in playful yet thoughtful acts of resistance. Sayraphim's book shows us all that we absolutely can MAKE the world a better place."

—**Rayna Fahey**, author of *Really Cross Stitch*

"Whether capturing stories in crochet or creating spontaneous interventions of crafted kindness, Sayraphim Lothian's projects show that the new resistance can be artistic, clever, and kind. Whether using street art or baking, embroidery or soft sculpture, she demonstrates that craftivism is at its very best a medium devoted to connecting humans together, one creative act at a time."

—**Leanne Prain**, author of *Strange Material: Storytelling through Textiles*; *Hoopla: The Art of Unexpected Embroidery*; and *Yarn Bombing: The Art of Crochet and Knit Graffiti* (with Mandy Moore)

"Sayraphim's *Guerrilla Kindness* brings people lost in the lonely whirlwind of modern times to a place of community, compassion, and connection. It's a wonder to watch how it affects people."

—**Lauren O'Farrell**, author of *Stitch London*, *Stitch New York*, and *Knit The City*

"Sayraphim's work is both thoughtful and playful; and most importantly, it makes the world a better place. I haven't had so much fun expressing my rage since throwing an egg at my father in '93. I love every one of Sayraphim's craft projects and adore the passion behind them. The craft room is the new war bunker, and Sayraphim Lothian is its field marshal. Badges not bombs! Finally, crafts that people are actually gonna give a shit about."

—**Claire Hooper**, host of *The Great Australian Bake Off*

"Lothian is an expert when it comes to creating whimsical interruptions to our daily lives."

—**Frances Atkinson**, author of *The Age*

"Sayraphim uses her craftivism to connect us to each other, to our community, and to creativity. Every project of hers I have been involved with has given me a sense of belonging and joy. Through her craftivism, Sayraphim teaches us how to tell our stories, create our dreams, and uncover hidden talents. Her work has inspired me to thread the eyes of needles, share stories with strangers I'll never meet, and learn about the wonders of ground-dwelling parrots in New Zealand."

—**Daniel Donahoo**, author of *Idolising Children* and *Adproofing Your Kids*; ex-blogger, *Geek Dad*

"Sayraphim has been one of the major craftivism proponents in Australia, activating craftivism's potential locally through her broad range of generous and uplifting projects. Her book is sure to inspire the next generation to embrace the political and personal benefits of crafting with intent!"

—**Dr. Kate Just**, artist, writer, and academic

"Sayraphim is one of the most dedicated stalwarts in the Melbourne craftivist scene. Over the last decade, she's carved a gently subversive oeuvre for herself that bridges the gap between traditional and radical craft and connects communities. Her work has provided an inspiration and a point of entry for hundreds of craft novices and seasoned crafters who want to play with the boundaries of their art forms and their potential to express ideas. Always seeking to be playful, inclusive, and progressive, Sayraphim's new book, *Guerrilla Kindness and Other Acts of Creative Resistance*, is set to be essential reference material for curious craftivists from all walks of life."

—**Casey Jenkins**, craftivist and artist

"Sayraphim.is one of Australia's leading craftivists. With a background in theatre, film, television, street games, and public art, Sayraphim brings her unique combination of performativity and generosity to bear on each of her creative forms, producing gentle and moving acts of creative resistance. Sayraphim's art serves as playful, compelling reminders of the power of making and of giving—they call us to be better to ourselves, to each other and to the world around us. This book is a must for anyone who loves to make, and who seeks inspiration to make a more compassionate world though the art of craft."

—**Dr. Cathy Hope**, Director of Play, Creativity, and Culture Project, Centre for Creative and Cultural Research, University of Canberra

This book was written on the traditional country of the Wurundjeri people in Australia and printed on Seminole land in the United States of America.

Aboriginal and Torres Strait Islander people are warned that this book may contain the names of deceased people.

CONTENTS

Foreword
by Betsy Greer

We live in a world where we hear and see hundreds of messages per day that tell us we are not good enough, thin enough, or pretty enough; messages that tell us we need to fix ourselves, and that we can't possibly be perfect the way we are right now. In any society where these messages persist, kindness, whether to ourselves or others, is an act of resistance and subversion. And it is from this place that I believe this book was born and is perhaps meant to live, from a place where your creativity radiates from within, and when it is acted upon and offered up, it shines on those around you.

I'm not much of a gardener, but when I make things and give them to others, either those unknown to me or much loved by me, I become one. I'm passing forward my belief in a world that is full of moments enriched by kindness, I'm handing off the idea that there is magic in the everyday, I'm helping others improve their perhaps otherwise dreary Monday. In a world where handmade things can be easily replaced by machine-made things, these self-made gifts are not only acts of love and devotion, they are testaments to the benefits of taking time out to get creative.

For years I have been inspired by Sayraphim's whimsical projects, which tend to have an eye on connecting with others in quiet and resonant ways. To me, this place of connecting without words is where we can plant seeds with our work. We can drop bits of resonance that can germinate into all sorts of very good things. This can be illustrated by what happens when one finds a gift left behind for a passerby to find, such as in Sayraphim's project, *For You, Stranger*. It's a jolt to the system, this finding of a beautiful object left on purpose in a world hell-bent on selling you things. There's no catch, no list to join lurking in the shadows, it's there for you, just as it says on the tag. In that moment where you dare to ask, "For whom?" and then even uncertainly answer it with "For me," you are quietly, almost imperceptibly, acknowledging that yes, you are worthy of this thing before you.

There is delight in the taking, but there is joy in the finding, the discovering. And these tiny bits of joy can plant seeds that root down deep into your system. They may grow down into your feet as you take a new path home. They may curve up to your mouth as you give someone a compliment. They may touch your hands as you give a waiter just a little bit more of a tip. And from there, who knows where they will go?

These small acts of rebellion against a system that so often tells you negative things push back against all the moments of harm, and instead dare you to believe differently, because doing kind things and finding kind things disrupts the often-negative feedback loop that can play ceaselessly in one's head.

This kind of creative resistance can take on more forms than the felt cupcakes shown in this book, it can involve a multitude of skills and interests. I can think of no better guide through this terrain than Sayraphim, who has lived it the past few years. So as you read, take notice of how it feels to learn about how to better your surroundings and society in ways that are good. Later, as you make something with which to take part, notice that feeling then as well. Let these feelings nourish you down to the bone and fill you up as they work to dislodge the age-old timeworn messages about not measuring up, slowly replacing them with a million silent affirmations saying, "You are perfect."

And remember that kindness is neither an act of futility or passivity in today's cultural climate, for when the situation calls for it, it can be an act of resistance, hope, and nurturing.

Introduction

Craftivism ("craft" + "activism") is a growing worldwide movement where artists, activists, and the general public use their crafting skills for political purposes. Going to a protest or calling your local politician is no longer the only way to raise your voice.

From anti-war cross stitch protests to personalizing your urban environment via sneaky guerrilla knitting, craftivism presents opportunities to creatively express your dissent; from raising awareness about the gender pay gap through baking to guerrilla mosaics protesting the death penalty in the USA, craft has been and can be used to promote and subvert in the name of your cause.

Around the world, activists are making banners to take on marches, attaching small stitched protests to street signs, and weaving words through fences. People are knitting messages of hope into beanies and jumpers, stitching pleas for peace and understanding into blankets and handkerchiefs, and making handmade items to sell to raise money for charities.

All of this is craftivism. Craftivism is any use of craft that changes the world for the better.

The term "craftivism" was coined by Betsy Greer in 2003:

> "Craftivism is the practice of engaged creativity, especially regarding political or social causes. By using their creative energy to help make the world a better place, craftivists help bring about positive change via personalized activism. Craftivism allows practitioners to customize their particular skills to address particular causes."
>
> —Betsy Greer, craftivism.com

Of course, using craft for activist purposes isn't new—the Suffragette movement was doing it in the nineteenth century—but recently, in the early part of this century, more and more people are turning to sewing needles and crochet hooks to get the word out there. So I've written this book to share some of the skills I've used to make my activism creative and to suggest them as ways for you to do the same.

There are around 30 projects in this book, and each one can be customized for your cause. I'm not here to tell you what causes you should support, I'm here to help you promote the movements that are near and dear to your heart. Along the way, I'll highlight a bunch of causes out there and give you links to find out more if you're interested.

Every project in this book is pretty easy to do if you have a bit of crafting knowledge, and none of it takes any special tools. If this is the first time you've picked up sewing or knitting needles or a crochet hook, no problem! I've got you covered with illustrated step-by-step instructions in the appendix, where you'll also find a reading list of other great books if you want to expand your craftivism library.

Craftivism is about making the world a better place, one handmade object at a time. So if you're a crafter who wants to promote a cause or an activist who wants to make a creative protest, this book is for you. March forth and make, my friends!

Advice to someone just starting out in activism

My advice to you is just go out and do it. Don't wait for permission or to find someone else or a group to do it with. If you have the urge, go out and create, go out and make, go out and do! Change so often starts at a grassroots level, which is people in their houses and people on the street. For instance, if you're concerned about taxes or mining, you might start making protest banners to attach to buildings or fences. Perhaps you love animals, in which case you might consider knitting blankets for an animal shelter. Maybe you'd like to protest but aren't keen on the shouting and scuffles at rallies and marches. Instead, you might organize a peaceful knit-in where you gather people together to sit and knit and chat about the problem.

Your acts of craftivism can speak for you if you can identify whose attention you want to draw to the issue you're highlighting. Do you want to directly target the company you disagree with, are you trying to raise awareness in your community, or is it your wish to speak directly to those affected? Where are the people you want to communicate with going to be? Once you start figuring out what you want to say and who you want to say it to, you're well on your way.

Social media

Social media is an amazing tool in a craftivist's repository. With it, you and your cause can potentially reach many more people much more quickly than was possible for activists in early eras. Once you've made your piece (and installed it, if it's going somewhere specific), take a photo of it and upload the image to social media. That way, your friends and those who follow you can see what you're making and what you're concerned about. Remember to use hashtags too, so other people can find your work. You can hashtag the cause, and you can also use more general hashtags like #craftivism, #craftivist, #creativeactivism, #creativeresistance, or even #creativeresistancebook.

A super quick (and not at all comprehensive) history of creative resistance

Using craft skills in activism has been around for a long time. The suffragettes fighting to give women the right to vote at the turn of the twentieth century employed their creativity in service of their emancipation. They made protest banners and stitched sashes, sewed slogans onto their clothes and umbrellas, created crockery with mottos and images, made jewelry, composed songs, and sewed and baked hand-crafted items to sell to raise money for their cause.

Between 1973 and 1990, women in Chile living under the dictatorship of Augusto Pinochet made small fabric pictures (called "arpilleras" in Spanish for the burlap cloth often used for backing) that depicted their life under the regime. These arpilleras depicted food shortages, government brutality, unemployment, and torture, and also told the stories of their missing and murdered family members. The scraps of cloth incorporated into the works were often pieces of the missing people's clothing. The arpilleras were smuggled out of the country to help tell the world of the Chilean people's plight. In some cases, the arpilleras themselves were used as part of testimonies in front of Amnesty International's Truth Commissions and helped them build pressure to bring down Pinochet.

The Greenham Common Women's Peace Camp was a women's only protest camp in and around Greenham Common in England from 1981 to 2000. The protest was a response to the government's decision to close the common to the community and situate ninety-six American nuclear cruise missiles at the site. The women's crafty activism came in many forms during their nineteen-year protest. Much of their action focused on the nine-mile fence that ringed the perimeter, which they would decorate with clothes, banners, rainbows, toys, and photographs of their children. Some of the symbols that were used most commonly were woven webs of wool and yarn. The women would weave these webs through the fence, through trees and tents, and around bulldozers and machinery brought in to remove the camp; and the women even wove webs around themselves, tradesmen, and police. The women were often arrested and brought to court, where they would spend their time weaving webs to be installed when they got back to camp.

In Australia, there was Billboard Utilizing Graffitists Against Unhealthy Promotions, known by their acronym BUGA UP (bugger up). They were a group of activists working across Australia from 1979 to the mid-1980s who targeted billboards advertising tobacco and alcohol, modifying the slogans by painting out letters and adding others to raise awareness of the health concerns associated with the products advertised. Their members included doctors, health workers, journalists, and pensioners, and two of the BUGA UPers went on to become politicians in the New South Wales parliament. The BUGA UP campaign is on record as having been influential on the tobacco advertising debate, and in 1992 it became illegal to advertise tobacco in Australia.

There are, of course, loads more examples of people resisting creatively. A quick search of the hashtags #craftivism, #craftivist, #creativeresistance, and #artactivism (just to name a few!) will bring up thousands of people making amazing creative resistance works.

Problematic symbols

It's important before we begin to have a quick chat about symbols and their use. Symbols are a really good shorthand for an issue—a picture is worth a thousand words—and a symbol can instantly sum up what you're protesting and show what side you're on. But it's very important to research the symbols you intend to use to make sure you're familiar with their history and who has used them before you. Many symbols have been used to represent identity and community, or as signs of belonging and association, so an ignorant approach to them can falsely imply ownership or entitlement.

For instance, although the raised fist symbol has been used by many movements over the past one hundred years, it's most commonly associated with the Black Power movement in the USA and the Black Panther Party. The Black Panthers were an African American revolutionary party founded in 1966 by Huey Newton and Bobby Seale, which was originally formed to patrol black neighborhoods protecting the citizens from police brutality. Around the same time the women's liberation movement was making use of the women's symbol in protests, on fliers, shirts, and other items. It is believed that African American women first placed the two together, marching under banners which proudly displayed the Black Pride raised fist inside the women's symbol.

Some people argue that because of its origin that white people shouldn't use it, as it's a symbol created by and for use by black people only.

Another example is the Pussyhat Project, a knitted beanie project created for the Women's March in 2017. The creators, Krista Su and Jayna Zweiman, called for people to knit or crochet pink beanies with cat ears, "pussy hats," in response to misogynist comments made by the newly elected 45th president of the United States of America, Donald Trump. One train of thought is that because it uses the word "pussy," it alienates trans women because not every woman has a vagina. Other people object to the use of the color pink. They see the color as referring to white people's skin tone, and thus feel that the project and the symbol is exclusionary of people of color.

This is why it's important to research the symbols you plan to use in your activism. Know where they came from and who invented them, and be aware of and sensitive to the issues associated with them. That way you can decide for yourself where you stand on their use.

Identity politics

A hyper-realized fantasy of what it is to be a normal person is pervasive throughout the majority of mainstream western media. In films, on TV, in magazines, and in advertising, western society is saturated with the image of happy, successful, "normal" people depicted as straight, white, able-bodied, thin, and beautiful.

For everyone who is not white, straight, cisgender, thin, able-bodied, and young, the daily experience of being "othered" by this culture is unavoidable. In such a society, any person who identifies as a person of color, disabled, queer, or otherwise at all different from the "norm" exists permanently as an outsider.

Of course, not everyone wants to shout about their gender, sexuality, and/or racial identity from the rooftops—and it's not always safe to do so. But where it is safe, and when you feel up to it, you can be the person you need to see in the world.

Reclaiming words

A word about words. Words are like symbols; treat words the way you'd treat symbols. Know their history and how they're being used now. Particularly with words, be aware of the sensitivities that surround them. Know which words have been used as slurs or attacks in the past, which words belong to which communities, and what their use represents.

Sustainable activism

Personally, I try hard not to buy too many new products like fabric, yarn, and clothes. There's already so much stuff out there in the world. Instead, I try to buy as much stuff secondhand as I can. I've visited the charity shops around town so often in the past few decades that I now navigate my way around town by them. I've accumulated enough interesting fabric and materials that many of the materials for the projects in this book were created using secondhand materials from my stash. I'd encourage you to try to do this as well. If you head down to your local charity shop, flea market, or trash and treasure/ trunk sale, you'll be amazed at what's around to buy, usually at much cheaper prices.

For instance, quilts can be backed with single, double, or queen sized sheets, and quilt wadding can be made from secondhand blankets and towels. Toys and other fabric items can be made from cut up clothes, and there's always more yarn, knitting needles, and other odds and sods out there just waiting to be rehomed. While it is true that sometimes you need that one "perfect" thing that you have to buy from a fabric or art store, once you start looking you'll find a myriad of other interesting and sometimes unique or vintage materials out in the world just waiting for you.

Signing your work

Historically, a lot of women's work and craft work has been undervalued and ignored, and a contributing factor to this has been the lack of a signature or maker's mark on many of these works.

A famously typical example is the Bayeux Tapestry. No one knows who made the Bayeux Tapestry, a 230 foot (70 meter) long embroidered cloth telling the story of the Norman conquest of England in 1066. Experts aren't sure when it was created (possibly 1077), but the earliest known reference to it comes from 1476. Historians are fairly confident as to who commissioned it, but have no idea of the identity of the people who created the tapestry. Almost certainly all women, they must have spent close to a decade actually sewing it, but because there are no signatures on the piece and because it wasn't recorded who made it, their identities and their participation in the making of this work have been lost to history.

So it's always important to sign your craft work, especially if you're giving it as gifts. In a generation, how else will they know who made it and why?

A quick note about measurements

Throughout this book, I use both imperial and metric measurements. For those of you fluent in both, you'll notice that sometimes the conversions don't quite match up (for instance, 2 inches doesn't quite equal 5 centimeters). But that's okay; nothing in the book needs absolutely precise measurements. So, all conversions have been rounded up or down to the nearest quarter-inch or centimeter, which makes it easier for everyone.

Finished is better than perfect

And finally, a note about perfection. At best, it doesn't really exist, and at worst, it's unattainable, so don't worry about it! Perfection isn't something *you* see, it's something other people see. When you look at a piece you've made, you'll always see the faults, the wobbly lines, and the alternative color choices. Other people looking at your piece will marvel at the awesomeness of it, they'll be inspired by your creativity, and they'll learn about your cause. Don't get stuck in the pursuit of perfection, instead make your piece with joy and be done. Aiming for perfection means it'll live forever in your "work in progress" pile, waiting for you to keep fine-tuning it. Finished is better than perfect; finished means it can go out in the world and do its job.

CHAPTER ONE
Guerrilla Kindness

Guerrilla kindness combines the concept of guerrilla art with the idea of random acts of kindness. A work of guerrilla kindness involves making small handcrafted artworks and leaving them in the public spaces of cities around the world for random people to discover and take. The philosophy of the work, in short, is to practice random acts of guerrilla kindness to lift people's spirits and make them happy.

An act of guerrilla kindness is subversive; it's a tiny moment between two strangers; it's one person stepping up to change someone else's day, anonymously, sneakily, joyfully.

Kindness and joy themselves can be radical acts. So often contemporary capitalist culture reduces us to being bitchy and mean to each other. Trolling is rampant online, bullies threaten us in our childhoods and adulthoods, and even our parliamentarians have devolved into yelling school taunts instead of working towards getting anything done. When all around us our communities are tearing themselves apart with infighting and name-calling, it can fairly be asked how just being nice to strangers is activism.

Random acts of kindness are a rebellion against the expected and entrenched nastiness, and joy and confidence in yourself is a radical act. Every moment of radical kindness, guerrilla or otherwise, is an opportunity to deny the powerful the power of their ideology. When you give something precious away for free, you fly in the face of the assumptions of capitalism. When you take a moment to take care of yourself, you deny the propaganda of the patriarchy, with its constant repetition of images and structures that reinforce cis hetero male perspectives on femininity; these messages have the effect of suppressing difference from a toxically unattainable "ideal" and telling you that you are worthless but for the value placed upon you by others. In a moment of guerrilla kindness, these acts of generosity function like secret messages and whispered words of encouragement and solidarity.

A work of guerrilla kindness is "dropped" somewhere for someone to find. Usually, there is a tag attached to show finders that the work is free for the taking. When making your own guerrilla kindness work, consider: what will you write on the tag to invite people to take your gift? How will you indicate that this is a present for them? It needs to be short and sweet.

You can also put contact details on the tag—a Twitter handle, email address, or a hashtag like #guerrillakindness or #freeartfriday—to encourage the finder to let you know the work was found or to say thank you. But don't be disappointed if the finders don't report back. This isn't about demanding a reply; this is about creating a joyous, obligation-free moment of kindness.

Any of the projects in this book can be made into guerrilla kindness projects by simply leaving them out in public with a tag to let the finder know they are deliberate gifts and not abandoned objects. The following four projects, however, were all designed specifically as guerrilla kindness works.

Guerrilla Kindness Placement Tips

I've been making guerrilla kindness projects for close to ten years now, and I've come up with some guidelines I use to give them the best chance of being found.

- ❑ Try not to leave them somewhere too low or too high where people won't be able to see them.

- ❑ Don't leave them on rubbish bins or on the ground; people will assume they are trash and won't take them.

- ❑ Do leave them somewhere people are, like libraries, cafes, or busy streets.

- ❑ If you have social media, take a photo and upload it to help your followers find it.